Written by Shannon Richardson & Illustrated by Bonnie Lemaire

ISBN-13: 978-1540748805
ISBN-10: 1540748804
LCCN: 2016920192

CreateSpace Independent Publishing Platform
North Charleston, South Carolina

To my four children who, without their sarcasm and teasing (with love and affection) about my use of "big words" in children's books, I would have never added a rhyming glossary; one of the most enjoyed and appreciated aspects of my books ...it's also what prompted me to write a book about words.

There are many people who say,

some words are too grand;

Too Colossal

too Enormous

too Vast

to understand.

But that's simply not true, words are just talk;

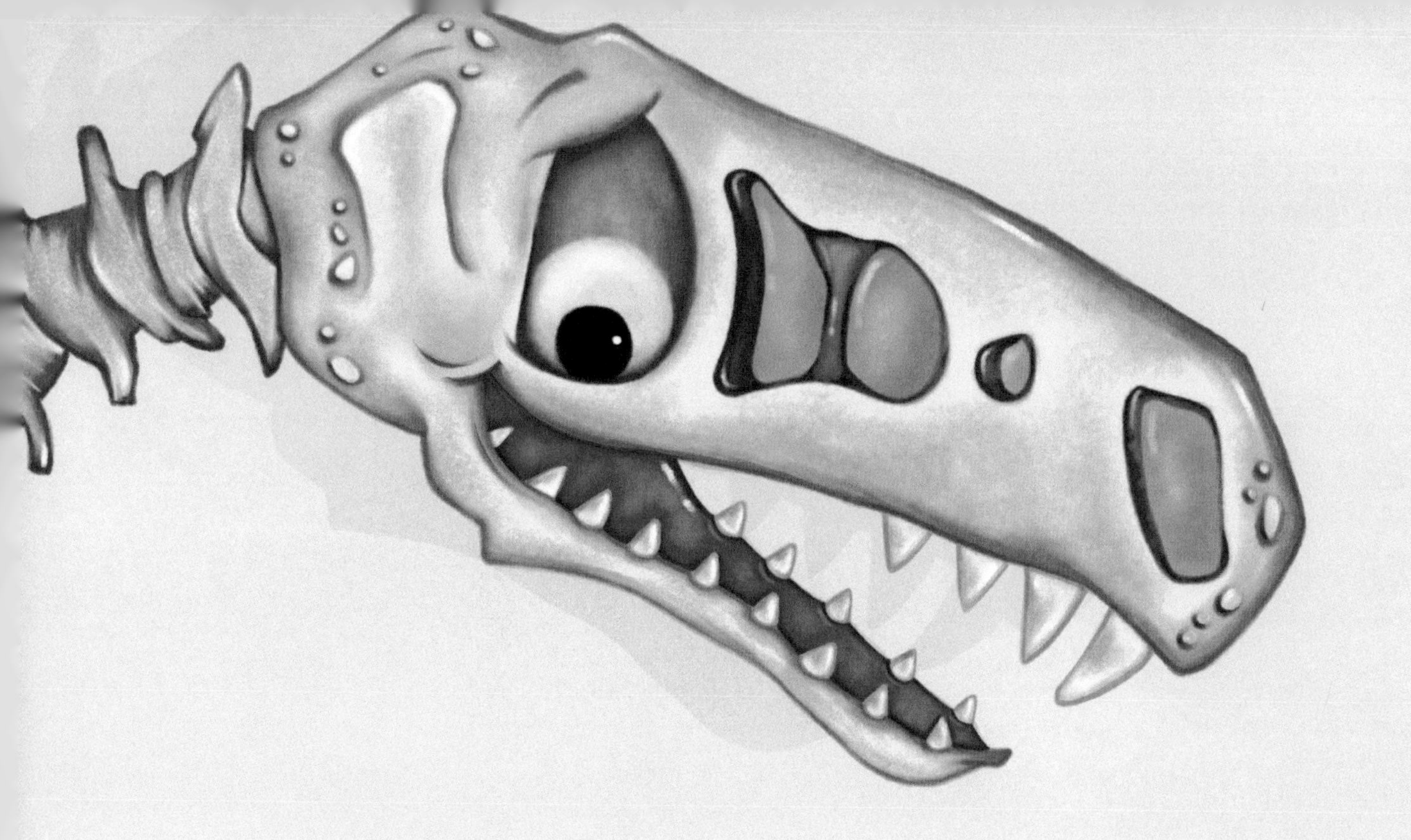

You were learning new words

before you could walk!

Words are just words, so don’t shy away;
Tools to help us figure out what to say!

WORDS
are just
WORDS

There are many words that roll–off the tongue;

are some!

Several

words

are hard to pronounce,

so you must take your time;

Miscellaneous,

superlative,

and words like

SUBLIME!

Some are exciting to say,
and a little silly too;
Like
sarsaparilla,
persnickety,
gorgonzola,
and hullabaloo!

Don't forget,

supercilious,

vociferous,

and haberdashery

are fun;

We're expanding your gray matter, and we're not even done!

Confounded,
flabbergasted, befuddled,
and perplexed;

You might feel this way,
you might feel quite vexed!

When learning new things it can be quite a dare;
But you're up for the task, you've got guts and flair!

There are thousands of words
just waiting to be said;
You need only to learn them,
then they're tucked in your head!

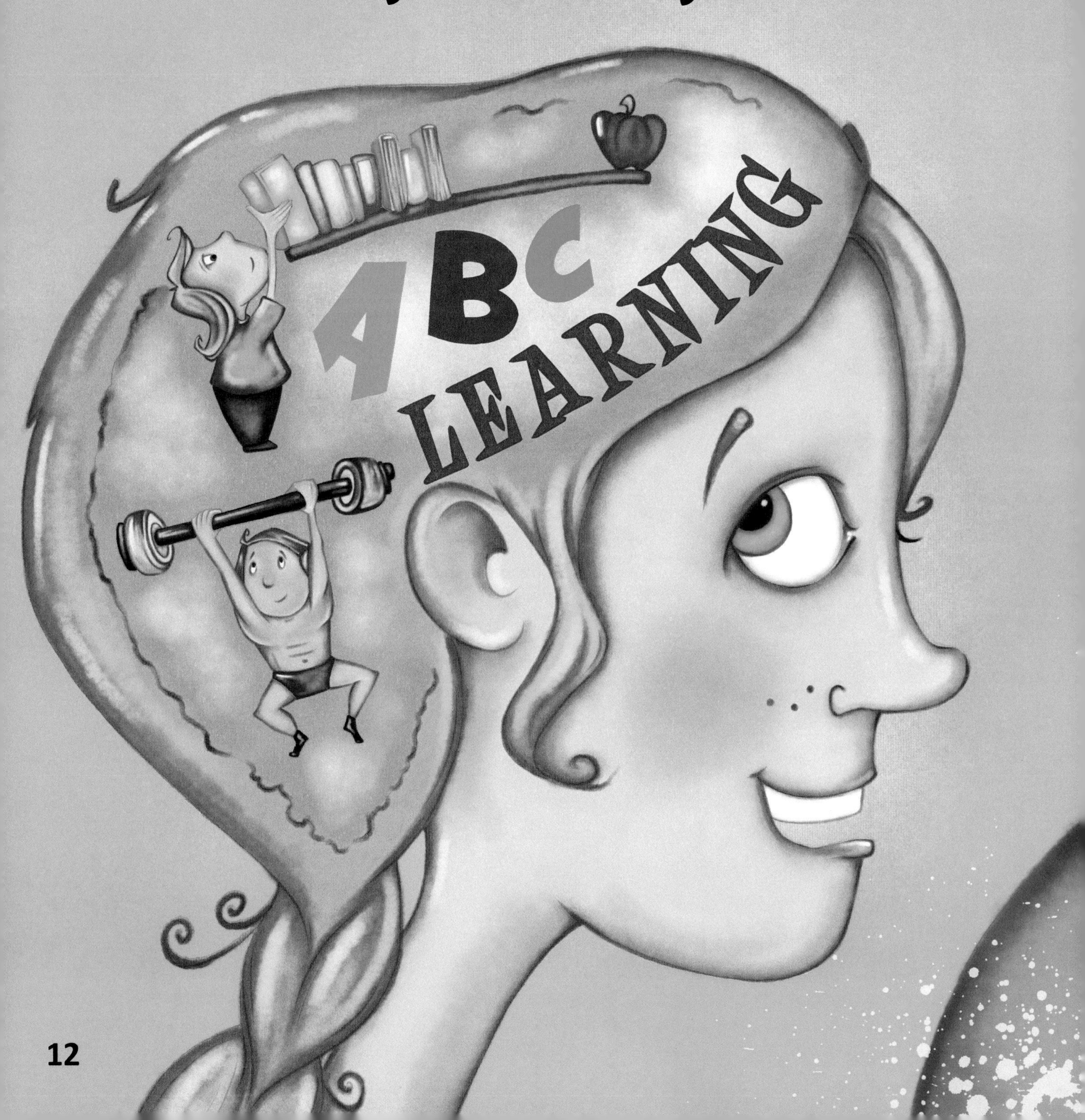

When you engage in conversation,
discussion, and speech;
They'll roll right out,
like a wave on a beach!

You're filling your brain with
information and knowledge;
Learning new things
from birth through college!

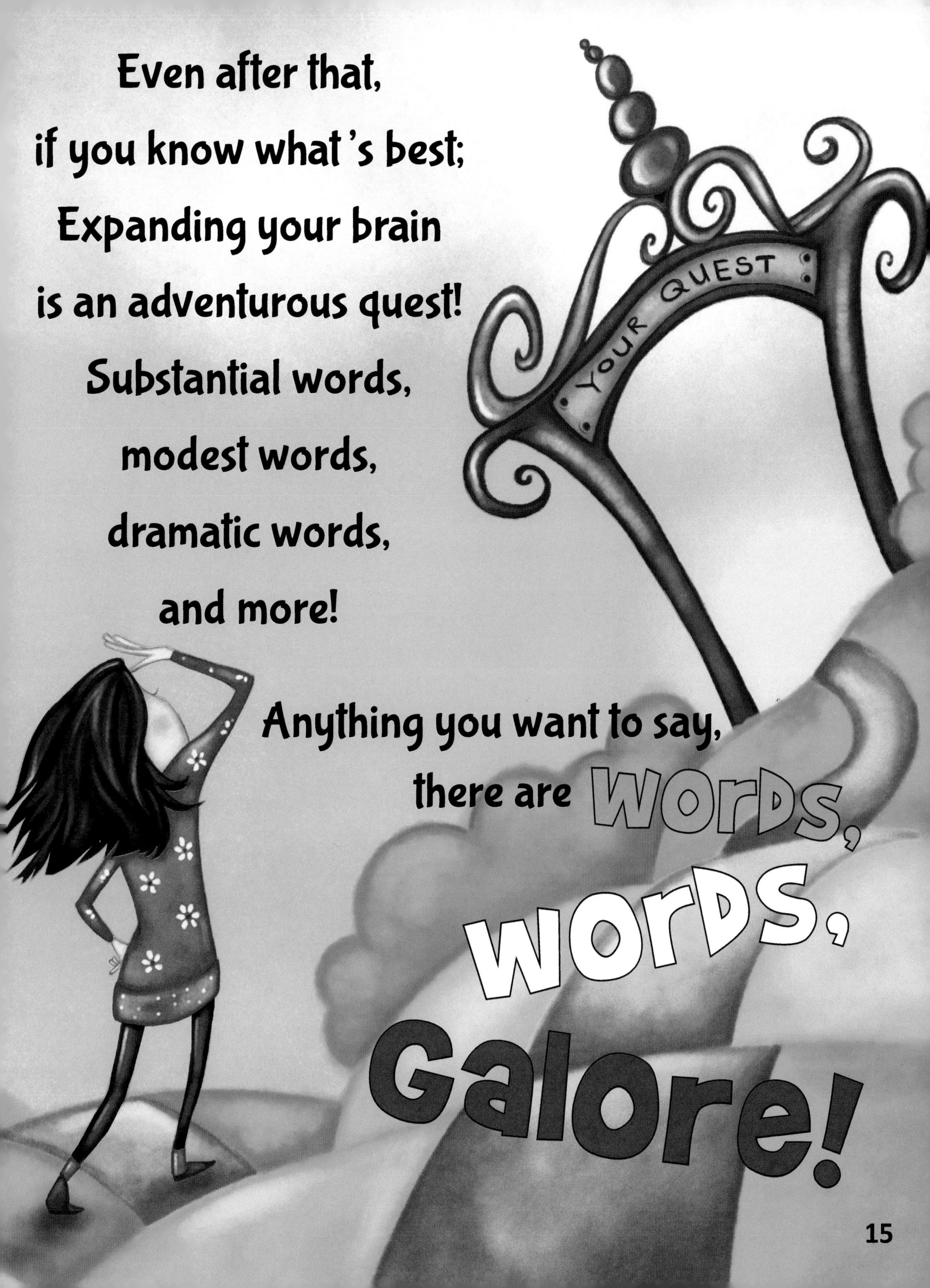

Even after that,
if you know what's best;
Expanding your brain
is an adventurous quest!
Substantial words,
modest words,
dramatic words,
and more!

Anything you want to say,
there are WORDS,
WORDS,
GALORE!

IRATE = angry,
Melancholy
means sad,
and
TIMID
is shy,

Exceptional
is special,
Repudiate,
Deny

See how fast you are learning,
no need to despair!

It happens quite quickly,
your know starts to grow;
Your lexis expanding
like a ball in the snow!
FRAY
HUBRIS
Perfunctory

If you feel a bit weary, and your head has an ache,

Go slow, take a breath, and maybe a break.

Learning new things can make you quite worn;

But, guess what?

You've been doing it since you were born!

The alphabet = letters, each letter has a sound;
Join letters to make words,
which make language profound.

Words convey feelings;
they communicate thoughts and aspiration;
They express...

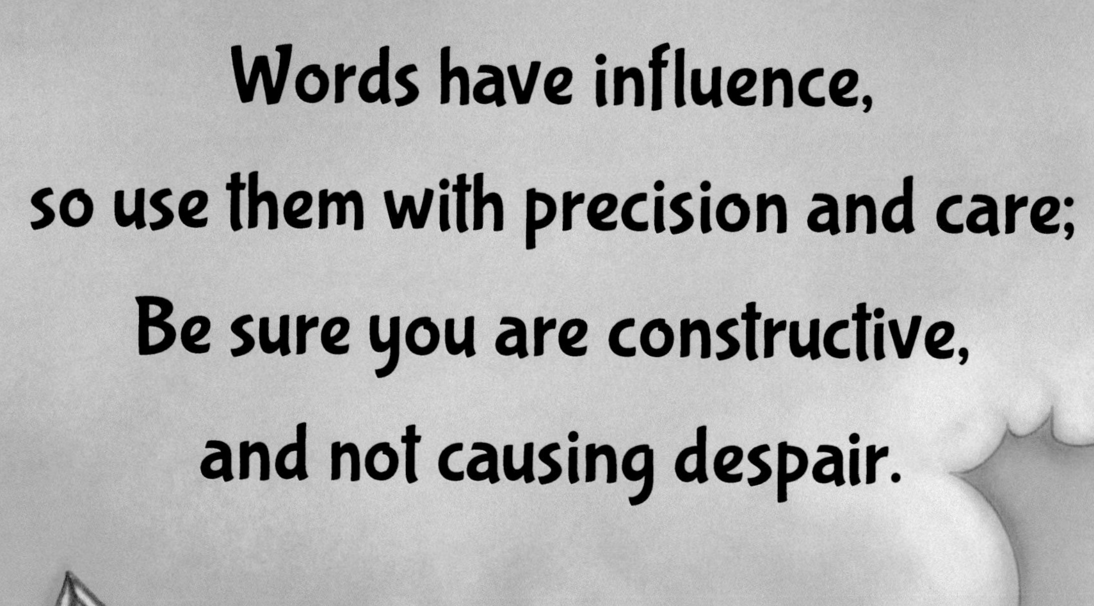

Words have influence,
so use them with precision and care;
Be sure you are constructive,
and not causing despair.

Words are just words ,
even the word "word" is a word;
Words you can 't learn?
That 's simply absurd!

It's everyday stuff,
these words and their meaning;
They were made just for us,
for learning and gleaning!

So now you are off,
you are well on your way,
To a word paradise
hip-hip-hooray!

Next time you face a word that seems scary,

Stare straight at that word,

do not blink, or be wary!

Sound it out slowly, there's no rush or haste;

Then look up the meaning,

your fear's now defaced!

You've learned a new word,
you can use as you choose;
You're growing your knowing,
no way can you lose!

You've tackled your fear with courage and zest;
Like Lewis and Clark on their journey out west!

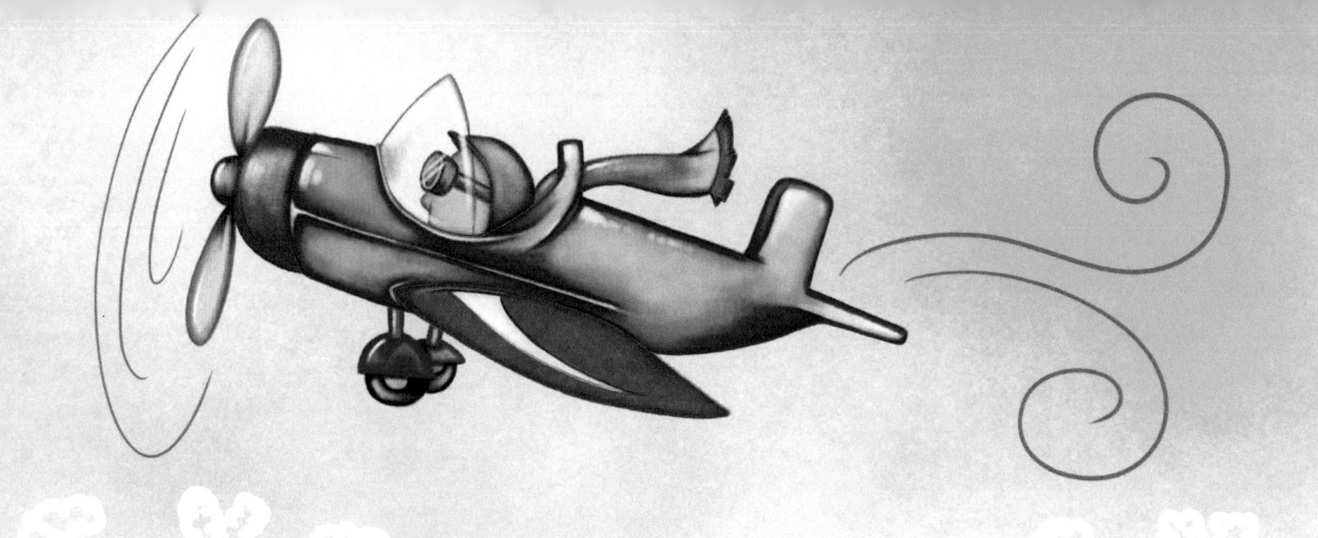

It's that time, we've come to the end of the book...but not the expedition!

Learning new words is a life-long mission!

See, aren't you glad you stepped onto this trail;
You cannot succeed if you are afraid you will fail.

Your understanding is growing,
your know is now knowing;
That words are just words
meant for learning, then sowing!

Glossary

Absurd: It's ridiculous, preposterous, silly, or bizarre; it most likely means you have gone too far!

Arrogance: Is conceit and smugness, people who are snobbish, and vain; their nose in the air, their presence a bane.

Aspiration: Is ambition, a goal, objective, or desire, purpose, and determination, all things to admire.

Befuddled: Puzzled, stumped, lost, or bemused; means you feel cloudy, mixed-up, and confused.

Colossal: Is huge, immense, gigantic, enormous, or great; like the heavens, or mountains, or vast desert landscape.

Confounded: Is mystified, puzzled, bewildered, and confused; but it also means defeated, irritated, annoyed…not amused!

Constructive: To build-up, encourage, effect value, not strife; be constructive, and loving to one-another in life.

Conundrum: Is a challenge, a problem, riddle, or mess; the product of which may sometimes cause stress.

Copasetic: It's agreeable, satisfactory, just ducky, or fine; it's all good, no problems, all worries behind.

Defaced: To demolish, spoil, teardown, or devastate; the opposite of build-up, construct, or create.

Despair: Misery, anguish, hopeless, gloom; it may wish to reside in your heart, but give it no room.

Enormous: Huge, vast, massive, titanic; like oceans, and mountains, and skies gigantic!

Expedition: Voyage, journey, mission, outing, or trek; like mountain climbing, or scuba diving on an old shipwreck.

Famished: Starving, hungry, having had nothing to eat; the opposite of full, satisfied, gorged, or replete.

Flabbergasted: Stunned, astonished, bowled over, or surprised; you could see she was flabbergasted by the look in her eyes.

Flair: Is a talent or skill, a gift, or a knack, ability, or intellect, things not to lack.

Fray: It is a dispute, a tussle, fight, or brawl; one should seek to rise above it all.

Frustration: Obstruction, aggravation, exasperation, feelings we wish to avoid; the opposite of success, satisfaction, or overjoyed.

Galore: Plentiful, abundant, profuse, like the stars in the sky, or the sands of the sea, or the mountaintops high.

Gleaning: Collecting, gathering, harvesting, or reaping; garnering, assembling, amassing, or heaping.

Gorgonzola: Is a cheese, and it's blue, it's a fun word to say, that's why I shared it with you!

Gray matter: Is the stuff in your brain where the thinking takes place; it can never be filled up, or run out of space!

Haberdashery: A shop that sells buttons, ribbons, zippers, patterns, and more; to a seamstress, or tailor, a quite purposeful store.

Haste: Speed, hurriedness, rush, are the same as haste; the practice of which can sometimes cause waste.

Hubris: Pride, arrogance, vanity, conceit; in love with one's self from their head to their feet.

Hullabaloo: It's a racket, a rumpus, an uproar of noise; those who partake have lost all their poise!

Influence: Motivate, impact, sway, or spur; your influence should be positive, most would concur.

Lexis: It's language, vocabulary, communication, we use it every day; it can be lyrics to a song, stories in a book, or a script for a play.

Millennium: Is a word to describe time, one-thousand years to be exact; one hundred decades, or twelve thousand months...two additional fun facts.

Miscellaneous: Means various, assorted, diverse, or unlike; as the leaves you might find in the woods on a hike.

Modest: Reserved, humble, restrained, or meek, the opposite of flashy, overbearing, or sleek.

Perfunctory: Is cursory, careless, hurried, a lack of enthusiasm, or passion; the teenager cleaned her room poorly, in a perfunctory fashion.

Perplexed: Is puzzled, mystified, stunned, or confused, baffled, bewildered, thrown-off, or bemused.

Persnickety: Means finicky, fussy, picky, perhaps hard to please; snooty types display it with ease.

Precision: Exactness, accuracy, done with meticulous care; she was fastidiously strict about the upkeep of her hair.

Profound: Is deep, thoughtful, insightful, or learned; when he witnessed the homeless, he was profoundly concerned.

Quest: Is a mission, a journey, expedition, or chase; like a voyage on a ship into deep outer space.

Sarsaparilla: Is a fun and sassy word to say; a soft drink for cowboys back in the day.

Serendipity: Is fortune, destiny, chance or fate; the opposite of purpose, design, or create.

Sowing: Is spreading, introducing, disseminating, or growing; like sharing new words to expand a friend's knowing!

Sublime: Is beautiful, inspiring, moving, or extolled; like breathtaking sunsets of orange, and gold.

Substantial: Extensive, ample, essential, big, or profuse; like the literary works of our friend Dr. Seuss!

Supercilious: They are people who are arrogant, snooty, and stuck-up, unfriendly, snobby with their noses turned up!

Superlative: Is excellent, unmatched, exceptional, great, outstanding, unbeatable, unquestionably first-rate!

Vast: Is massive, infinite, cosmic, or grand; like the number of grains in the ocean sand.

Vexed: Annoyed, irritated, aggravated, or cross; feelings you experience when at a loss.

Vociferous: Is loud, rowdy, noisy, or clamorous; her vociferous outburst was anything but glamorous!

Wary: It's suspicious, nervous, mistrustful, or restrain; he was wary of flying, so instead took the train.

Weary: Is tired, sleepy, exhausted, just beat! When you're drained of energy from your head to your feet!

Zest: It's enthusiasm, gusto, keenness, desire; wonderful passion, all things to admire.

Made in the USA
Middletown, DE
22 November 2019